DISCOVERING SEABIRDS

by Charis Mather

Minneapolis, Minnesota

Credits
All images are courtesy of Shutterstock.com, unless otherwise specified. With thanks to Getty Images, Thinkstock Photo, and iStockphoto. Recurring – Net Vector, Baskiabat, NotionPic, PCH.Vector, Latelier, Susann Guenther. Cover – sichkarenko.com, Petr Salinger, reisegraf.ch. 2–3 – Joshua Raif. 4–5 – Det-anan. 6–7 – Jodie Nash, Lina S. Punkz. 8–9 – SmallSnail, smtshn2, Stephen A. Waycott, Sudowoodo. 10–11 – Audra Thomson, Kathy Kay. 12–13 – Andrea Izzotti, WaceQ. 14–15 – Joanne Caffrey, Johnny Giese. 16–17 – iacomino FRiMAGES, Rudmer Zwerver. 18–19 – Imogen Warren, LouieLea. 20–21 – Agami Photo Agency, Andrea Izzotti. 22–23 – HannaTor, Steve Bower.

Bearport Publishing Company Product Development Team
Publisher: Jen Jenson; Director of Product Development: Spencer Brinker; Managing Editor: Allison Juda; Editor: Cole Nelson; Associate Editor: Naomi Reich; Associate Editor: Tiana Tran; Designer: Kim Jones; Designer: Kayla Eggert; Designer: Steve Scheluchin; Production Specialist: Owen Hamlin

Library of Congress Cataloging-in-Publication Data is available at www.loc.gov or upon request from the publisher.

ISBN: 979-8-89577-025-2 (hardcover)
ISBN: 979-8-89577-456-4 (paperback)
ISBN: 979-8-89577-142-6 (ebook)

© 2026 BookLife Publishing
This edition is published by arrangement with BookLife Publishing.

North American adaptations © 2026 Bearport Publishing Company. All rights reserved. No part of this publication may be reproduced in whole or in part, stored in any retrieval system, or transmitted in any form or by any means, electronic, mechanical, photocopying, recording, or otherwise, without written permission from the publisher. Bearport Publishing is a division of FlutterBee Education Group.

For more information, write to Bearport Publishing, 3500 American Blvd W, Suite 150, Bloomington, MN 55431.

CONTENTS

All Aboard! 4
For Your Information . . . 6
Gulls. 8
Pelicans 10
Cormorants 12
Fulmars 14
Puffins 16
Albatrosses 18
Frigatebirds. 20
Back on Land! 22
Glossary 24
Index 24

ALL ABOARD!

Ahoy there! Welcome aboard my ship. I am Captain Gulliver of the See-Gulls Ocean Tours. My crew and I are happy to have you along for our journey!

CAPTAIN GULLIVER

FOR YOUR INFORMATION

There are more than 300 different kinds of seabirds. These birds have **adapted** to life around the ocean. Many seabirds even have special **glands** that allow them to drink salt water.

Salt water is fine for me but not for you. So, don't drink it!

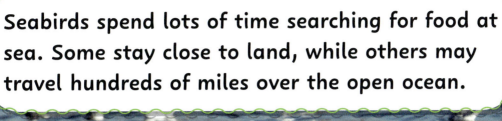

Seabirds spend lots of time searching for food at sea. Some stay close to land, while others may travel hundreds of miles over the open ocean.

Fishers sometimes follow seabirds to find fish.

GULLS

This gull told me about a new seafood spot!

Gulls are a noisy bunch. They use their calls to **communicate** with one another. Different calls may have different meanings. They could warn of danger or share the location of food.

PELICANS

Pelicans are great hunters. These seabirds scoop up fish with their large, stretchy **bills**. Then, they lean their heads forward to drain the water. Finally, pelicans swallow the fish whole.

That looks like a tasty fish!

Because pelicans spend lots of time in the water, they have to make their wings **waterproof**. These birds spread a special waterproof oil, called preen oil, through their feathers.

Pelicans make preen oil in a gland near their tails.

CORMORANTS

Cormorants do not have large bills to scoop up fish. Instead, these seabirds dive underwater to get food. Cormorants can dive as deep as 150 feet (45 m).

Bring some back for me!

While underwater, cormorants kick their large, **webbed** feet to swim. They use their wings to help steer toward a fishy meal.

Cormorants can hold their breath for more than two minutes.

FULMARS

Many seabirds fly close to the water's surface while searching for their next meal. However, fulmars hunt with more than their eyes. These birds use their powerful sense of smell to sniff out fish, squid, and more.

Scientists think fulmars can smell things that are up to 15 miles (25 km) away.

Fulmars spend most of their lives at sea. When it is time to have young, however, they head to rocky seaside cliffs to make their nests. How do these birds stay safe? Fulmars spit a stinky oil at **predators** to keep them away!

Plug your nose, and don't get too close!

PUFFINS

Like fulmars, puffins also make nests along cliffs to lay eggs and raise chicks. When they are not nesting, puffins are swimming or hunting out at sea.

Puffins have large orange, black, and yellow **beaks.** Their mouths are big enough to hold many small fish at once, which they carry back to nests for their young to eat.

Puffins have jagged tongues that keep fish from slipping out.

ALBATROSSES

Albatrosses can soar through the air without flapping. They catch the wind under their wings and glide for hours at a time. This helps them save **energy** while at sea.

Albatrosses can travel almost 10,000 miles (16,000 km) without stopping.

18

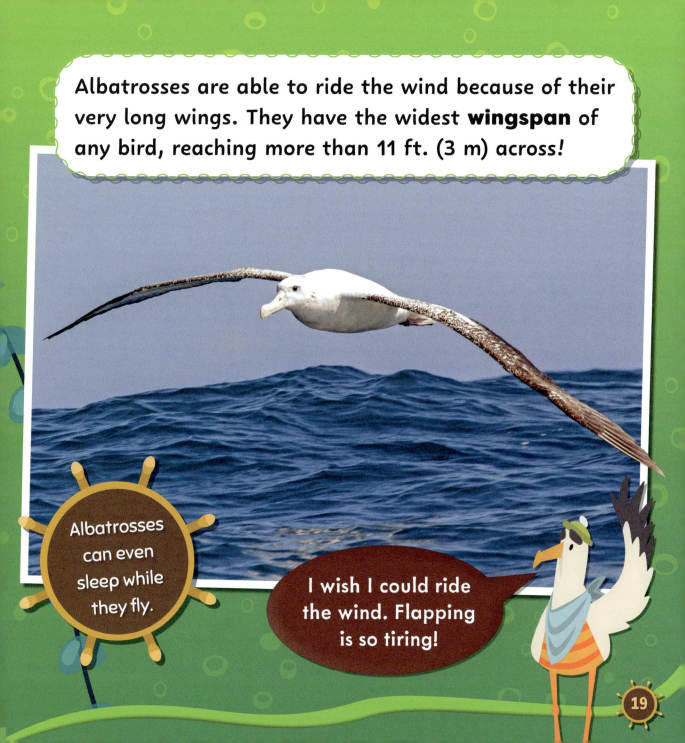

Albatrosses are able to ride the wind because of their very long wings. They have the widest **wingspan** of any bird, reaching more than 11 ft. (3 m) across!

Albatrosses can even sleep while they fly.

I wish I could ride the wind. Flapping is so tiring!

FRIGATEBIRDS

Like many seabirds, frigatebirds spend long stretches in the air. In fact, they can stay in the air for months at a time.

Frigatebirds have short legs and small feet that make it difficult for them to walk on land.

These seabirds do not have waterproof feathers, so they don't dive for fish. Instead, frigatebirds steal from other birds or catch fish and squid that come to the surface.

BACK ON LAND!

That is all the time we have for our tour today. Let's head back to land. We hope you enjoyed learning about some amazing seabirds!

GLOSSARY

adapted changed over time in order to survive in new surroundings

beaks hard, pointy mouthparts

bills the beaks and jaws of birds

communicate to share information with others

energy the power needed by all living things to move and stay alive

glands body parts that make substances or do useful jobs in the body

predators animals that hunt and eat other animals

waterproof able to stop water from getting through

webbed connected by thin skin

wingspan the distance between the tips of the wings

INDEX

beaks 17
bills 10, 12
cliffs 15–16
energy 18
feathers 11, 21
fish 7, 9–10, 12–14, 17, 21
nests 15–17
oil 11, 15
spit 15
tongue 17